Mules

Winsome Pinnock was born in London in 1961. Her plays include *The Wind of Change* (Half Moon Theatre, education tour, 1987), *Leave Taking* (Liverpool Playhouse Studio, 1988, National Theatre, 1995), *Picture Palace* (Women's Theatre Group, 1988), *A Hero's Welcome* (Women's Playhouse Trust at the Royal Court Theatre Upstairs, 1989), *A Rock in Water* (Royal Court Young People's Theatre at the Theatre Upstairs, 1989) and *Talking in Tongues* (Royal Court Theatre Upstairs, 1991). Her television credits include contributions to serials including *Chalk Face* (BBC2) and *South of the Border* (BBC1), and the screenplay *Bitter Harvest* (co-written with Charles Pattinson for BBC2 in 1992). Awards include the George Devine Award, Thames TV Playwrights' Scheme Award for Best Play of the Year 1991, runner-up Susan Smith Blackburn Prize, and the Unity Trust Theatre Award.

Mules was commissioned by Clean Break Theatre Company.

Set up by two women in Askham Grange prison in 1979, Clean Break produces high quality, original theatre which provides a powerful and unique voice for women prisoners, ex-prisoners and ex-offenders.

Mules received a workshop as part of the 1995/6 New Works Festival at the Mark Taper Forum, Los Angeles, California. Gordon Davidson artistic director/producer.

D1514094

For Oliver Mayer

With thanks to Olga Heaven, Hibiscus London; Merle Dawkins, Hibiscus Jamaica; Tom Shearin, women and staff of Holloway Prison, London; women and staff of Fort Augusta Prison, Jamaica; Vivia Pinnock, Hanif Kureishi and Lisa Petersen

Characters

Allie, teens, a runaway
Lou and Lyla, sisters, twenties, Jamaican
Bridie, drug courier, American
Rog and Sammie, Bridie's colleagues, English
Pepper, thirties
Piglet, twenties
Olu, Nigerian, illegal immigrant
Bad Girls 1 and 2
Rose, Allie's landlady

*This text went to press before the opening night and may
therefore differ from the version as performed*

Mules was commissioned by Clean Break Theatre Company and was first performed at the Royal Court Theatre Upstairs on 25 April 1996 with the following cast:

Lyla ⎫
Rog ⎬ Sheila Whitfield
Allie ⎭

Lou   ⎫
Sammie   ⎪
Pepper   ⎬ Abi Eniola
Olu   ⎪
Bad Girl 1 ⎭

Bridie   ⎫
Piglet   ⎪
Rose   ⎬ Clare Perkins
Bad Girl 2 ⎭

Directed by Roxana Silbert
Designed by Naomi Wilkinson
Lighting by Tanya Burns

Act One

London. An office.

Bridie What about Lorraine? She's available.

Rog She doesn't like Amsterdam.

Bridie What do you mean? She's never been to Amsterdam.

Rog She doesn't like the idea of it. She's a bit picky that one. I've got to be ever so careful about her assignments. I wouldn't indulge her, only she's so damn good.

Bridie Call her. Tell her to get her arse into gear. There's a flight booked this afternoon and I want her on it.

Rog She won't like it. (*She taps on portable phone.*)

Bridie She's not supposed to like it. This is a business, not a travel agency. And get her to do something about her hair. Last time I saw her she looked ridiculous. Why does the pursuit of glamour always begin with big hair?

Rog First things first, Bridie. I'll get her to say 'yes' to Amsterdam, then I'll tackle the hair.

Sammie I'm fucked.

Bridie I wouldn't say so.

Sammie Well and truly fucking shafted.

Rog She ain't there. It's the answerphone.

Bridie She's screening. Leave a message.

Sammie If I get my hands on that fucking bitch . . .

Bridie Stand in line, Sammie.

I

Sammie D'you ever see her Bridie? Fucking dope, educational subnormal, if I weren't so upset, I'd be in hysterics.

Rog Got her. (*She goes back to talking into the phone quietly.*)

Sammie Imagine, Bridie, she's hanging on to my every word like some love struck protégée and all the time, behind that pie-eyed look, she's scheming to get one over on me. I can't believe it.

Bridie I understand you're upset, Sammie, but right now we've got to deal with more pressing concerns than your loss of face.

Sammie Cliveden's gonna kill me.

Bridie Cliveden's not going to find out about this.

Sammie Ever since he started that MBA programme he's been poking his nose into every little nook and cranny. Feel like I'm being watched all the time.

Bridie Even if I have to replace that lot with money out of my own pocket, he's not going to find out, Sammie. Otherwise we're all fucked.

Rog gets off the phone.

Rog She won't go. Reckons she's got 'flu.

Sammie What am I gonna do, Bridie, I can't lose this job. I can't do anything else. Can you see me working at Woolworth's?

Bridie Give me the phone.

Rog You all right, Sammie?

Sammie I can't believe that kid was capable of doing something like that.

Rog You almost have to admire it. I mean, how did she

get all them other girls to go with her? Makes you all glad she's gone don't it? With that kind of courage, she'd a been bossing us around in a couple of years.

Sammie Cliveden's gonna kill me.

Rog Bridie'll know what to do.

Sammie Bridie's an expert in optical illusion is she? Even Cliveden, a man who can barely count to ten, is gonna be able to tell that a large chunk of his stock's gone missing.

Rog Bridie'll sort it out.

Sammie Superwoman to the rescue? She's not invincible, Rog.

Rog She's done it before.

Sammie Sabrina. Who'd'a thought I'd get shafted by someone called Sabrina.

Rog Makes you think, doesn't it.

Sammie About what?

Rog It just makes you think.

Sammie I tell you, Rog, I ever get my hands on her . . .

Bridie comes off the phone.

Bridie Have the new PA bike the tickets over to Lorraine.

Rog She's going?

Bridie Of course she's going. There you are, Sammie, problem solved.

Sammie What about Cliveden's little consignment?

Bridie Don't worry about it. He's got so much coming in all the time, shave a bit off here, a bit there. He'll be none the wiser.

Sammie You sure, Bridie?

Bridie It'll be fine. We'll rejig the schedule later.

Rog I'll get the kettle on in a minute. We've earned a cuppa.

Bridie A good morning's work I'd say.

Rog I thought we had a mutiny on our hands for a minute.

Bridie Women don't mutiny. They ask permission first.

Rog Sabrina didn't.

Bridie She's just stupid, stupidity makes you fearless.

Sammie Nothing flusters you, does it? I won't be able to relax until we're home and dry.

Bridie Come on, Sammie, we're much smarter than Cliveden. He just thinks he's the boss. I'd like to see him transform a bunch of adolescent schoolgirls into professionals.

Sammie You're right. I'm getting into a tiz about nothing.

Rog This place still haunted?

Bridie Three exorcisms and a spiritual douching by a voodoo priestess haven't managed to shift it.

Rog Bad luck. Years you've lived out of a suitcase, now you've decided to buy a house you pick a haunted one.

Bridie I've got that priest coming in again. That doesn't do it, I'll just have to move.

Rog My aunt May had a poltergeist, it was the spirit of a Welsh border collie that had belonged to the previous owner. The whole house shook every time a dog come on the telly. Christmas day was unbearable, what with all them repeats of *Lassie Come Home*.

Bridie This is some girl, apparently. Some poor dead girl. Nothing I can't deal with. What about that tea?

Rog I'm getting it. (*She goes.*)

Sammie Thanks, Bridie. I owe you one.

Bridie Don't worry, I won't let you forget it.

SCENE TWO

London. A bedsit.
  Rose, the landlady, enters the room with Allie.

Rose As you can see, it's not too dark for a basement flat. Darker today than usual, but that's because it's raining. There's a park round the corner and the shopping centre's only five minutes away. It's very easy for the centre of town. This being so self-contained you can come in any time of the night or day and not disturb the other tenants. As you can see, it's just been freshly decorated.

Allie Who had the room before?

Rose Some young girl. She left rather suddenly. Left the place in an awful state. You know what young people are like.

Allie I'll take it.

Rose You will?

Allie You sound surprised.

Rose I thought you said this was the first place you'd seen, that you might want to look around.

Allie I make my mind up very quickly and I've taken to this room.

5

Rose You have?

Allie It's got an atmosphere.

Rose Has it?

Allie Two hundred pounds deposit, wasn't it? (*Takes out wad of cash.*)

Rose Don't you want to think about it?

Allie It is up for rent, isn't it?

Rose Been on the market for several weeks. I haven't been able to shift it. I was beginning to think that my neighbours had been warning potential tenants off.

Allie Why would they do that?

Rose You know what neighbours are like. Malicious. I haven't spoken to her on the left since 1967 when her poodle met with an unfortunate accident in my back garden. Well, he shouldn't have been there in the first place, should he? As for her on the right, she's got her nose so far in the air, her feet don't touch the ground. Truth is, they're dying to see me leave this street. That's the way of the world we live in today, isn't it?

Allie Two hundred pounds deposit.

Rose To set against damage or breakages or returnable on departure.

Allie And a hundred pounds – two weeks in advance.

Rose Got a job have you?

Allie Waitressing in a restaurant on Oxford Street. We get huge tips.

Rose When were you thinking of moving in?

Allie Right now, if that's all right with you. Everything I need is in this case.

Rose You seem to know what you want. I'll leave you to it then, shall I? Anything you need, just give me a call.

Allie Thanks.

Rose goes. Allie walks around her home, savouring being alone in a room that she temporarily 'owns'. There is a knock on the door.

Olu Let me in. Please.

Allie Who is it?

Olu A neighbour. I saw you come in. I want to welcome you.

Allie lets Olu into the room. Olu more or less tumbles in. She walks around the room, very agitated. Nervous and edgy.

Just moved in? I live downstairs. This room is much nicer than mine. You're very young to be living alone.

Allie I'm very independent for my age.

Olu You're not from London?

Allie No.

Olu And your parents trusted you to come to London by yourself?

Allie My parents trust me, yeah.

Olu My parents barely let me go out shopping on my own. Of course, things are very different in Nigeria. Where did you get all that money?

Allie Who wants to know?

Olu You stole it, didn't you?

7

Allie I saved it. I don't believe in stealing.

Olu Lend me some money?

Allie You what?

Olu Twenty pounds will do.

Allie Push off. After I've paid the rent I won't have enough for myself.

Olu You must be able to spare twenty pounds.

Allie Why should I give you any money? I don't know you.

Olu You've run away from home, haven't you? So have I, although my home is a long way away. You have very soft skin.

Allie Look you, this is my room and if you don't get out I'm going to call the landlady.

Olu Let me have some of your face cream. I look like fifty years old. Guess how old I am. Go on.

Allie I don't know.

Olu I am twenty-two. Twenty pounds.

Allie I haven't got twenty pounds. I gave everything I have to Rose.

Olu Fish around in your pockets.

Allie Nothing, look.

Olu I haven't eaten for four days. Please. You may need someone to spare you a few coppers one day.

Allie No disrespect . . . (*Searches for Olu's name.*)

Olu Olu.

Allie No disrespect, Olu, but you stink.

Olu Rats stink, don't they? That's what they call us run-aways, rats.

Allie I'm not a runaway.

Olu Then why do you have such a small suitcase? You left in a hurry.

Allie This is my room. I've got a key, see. You're not allowed in unless I invite you. Tomorrow I'm gonna get me a job waitressing in a restaurant, I'll get me a nice crisp uniform with a big pocket for customers' tips – I ain't no stinking rat.

Olu I am a runaway myself. From Nigeria, the underground. They get you false papers, passports. They organize everything, but they certainly make you earn the favours they do you. That's why I'm in the state I am now. Do you have any moisturizer? My skin is so dry. How old would you say I looked? Twenty-nine? Thirty-one? Guess again. You wouldn't believe what they made me do. They made me smuggle drugs. Yes. Made me insert packets of coke into my vagina. I had to do about thirty runs before they considered that I had repaid my debt. I hate to look so bad. I always took pride in the way I looked, even back in Nigeria I would find something, some oil, a little bit of butter, and keep my skin looking clean and healthy. In my vagina they made me smuggle those drugs and then when they had no use for me they left me to fend for myself. I haven't eaten properly for a week. Not even chips. I've been very ill lately. I think I may have TB or something. Last night I coughed up blood. Your skin is so soft. I'll bet you use expensive moisturizers. So soft. I bet you have never been in trouble in your life.

Allie I think you should leave my room now.

Rose comes into the room with a broom.

Rose Oh my God. How the hell did you get in here? You haven't got a key still, have you?

Olu She invited me in for supper.

Allie I didn't.

Rose No wonder my neighbours want to get rid of me. Go on, get out.

Olu Please, just 20p for a cup of tea.

Rose I hope you ain't given her nothing. It only encourages her. She'll only be back for more. Go on, get out, scram, you filthy little . . .

Olu Your meanness will find you out.

Rose Or do you want me to call the police?

Olu Your children are going to be born with rats' tails; as you treated me so you will one day be treated. Now I give you your fate.

Rose (*shooing Olu out with broom*) Oh God, not the old Nigerian curse trick. Get out of my house.

   Olu is gone.

Rose Have to have a spray around in here. Sorry you had to put up with that. You'll see a lot more of it before you've been here too long, that's for sure.

Allie I hate people like that. She was filthy.

Rose Cross the road to avoid it, wouldn't you? Don't ask what she's done to herself, that one, to be in that state.

Allie You'd think they'd have a bit more pride.

Rose And the excuses they come out with.

Allie We've all had it hard, in't we, but I'd never let myself get so low.

Rose She tell you her sob story then?

Allie Even if I had run away, I'd make sure I was still well turned out, clean and tidy.

Rose Stay away from types like her. You give her any money?

Allie I'm not that stupid.

Rose Drink, drugs and God knows what else she's into. I'd feel sorry for her if I didn't think she'd brought it all on herself. There but for the grace of God go we, Allison. All the advice I'm giving you is to keep your nose clean. Do that and you'll do very well here.

SCENE THREE

Kingston, Jamaica. A market.
  Music: reggae, upbeat. Lou and Lyla have set up a 'stall'. As they 'higgle' (sell their wares) they shout very loudly, trying to draw attention to their goods.

Lyla Come lady, come, come closer. You have X-ray vision? Come up close nuh man?

Lou Satin an' silk. Soft as milk. Underwear from Marks and Spencer, Englan'.

Lyla Quality, style and comfort. Bespoke brassières made to measure. (*under her breath to Lou*) Her titty look like it need a scaffold to hold it up.

Lou Yes, ma'am, I am a trained mammologist. Received my training from Macy's, New York. If you just step this way, ma'am, I will measure you up and fit you wit' a bra that will give you the perfect shape.

Lyla Naomi Campbell herself wear knickers like this.

(*under her breath*) An' by the look a them, this is the very baggy Naomi wear.

Lou If is good enough fe Naomi, is good enough fe all a we.

Lyla (*at the top of her voice, to an imaginary child*) Tek you filthy hand off a me drawers. Scram, you dirty little thief. What you want with a pair a woman panty? Nasty little wretch. Tha's right, ma'am, come and have a look.

Lou She say look. She never say touch. How you would like it if me put me hand inna fe you drawers?

Lyla nudges Lou. Hands on hips, they both watch an imaginary person walking by.

Lyla Watch her, nuh. A step as if she come from Beverly Hills.

Lou Watch her a wine and a twist she batty like a roller-coaster ride on a holiday Monday.

Lyla Don't bother a turn you nose up after we underwear because we ain't got nuttin' big enough fe batty like yours.

Lou You mouth too coarse you know, Lyla. You a go drive 'way the customers.

Lyla Which a customer? You see any customer?

Lou Exactly. A sell we a sell, you know. You have to speak nice to the people.

Lyla You nuh see me a speak nice to them? This way, modom. Why don't you buy a pair a Naomi Campbell soil up baggy?

Lou You got no sense a business, Lyla.

Lyla Who want buy a second-hand brassière?

Lou I think we should leave the selling to me.

Lyla Why?

Lou Because I was always the one that was good with words. You can take the money.

Lyla From now on, I will not bespeak until I am bespoken to.

Lou You have to make the people them feel like them the most important person in the world, like you glad as hell to see them. Flatter them, boost them. Loosen them and them will loosen them wallet.

Lyla This way, sir. I am so happy to see you. The sun come out the same time you smile. But what a way you bald head shiny and nice. You must stay up all night waxing it wit red carnival polish. Handsome? You make Denzil Washington look like donkey backside. Now, you a go buy me baggy or you just a go stand up and look?

Lou You out a order, Lyla. You want start fight in a market? You mother never teach you any manners?

Lyla We drink manners, milk outa the same bubby, didn't we, sister?

Lou But I always drink first – the sweetest cream always on the top. You did have to suck up the milk water me left behind. Is why everything come outa fe you mouth have a kind a stench while fe me words like a fragrant bouquet. (*to an imaginary person*) Will you get you ras clot backside outa fe we pitch? You nuh see you a trample pon we goods?

Lyla Fragrant? Bouquet? Aromatic fe sure.

They both laugh. Lou starts to pack up.

What you doing?

Lou We nah sell nuttin'. Might as well go back home.

Lyla Me did tell you say Kingsley offer me two score a melon? Cut up some a that melon in slices, juice up the rest with ice. In this weather, we soon make a selling.

Lou I know what sorta overripe fruit that Kingsley a go give we. Slice it open you see a heap a maggot jumping carnival.

Lyla So we just a go stand out here getting suntan every single day?

Lou We need to restock.

Lyla An' how we a go do that?

Lou Go to Miami, ennit?

Lyla An' how we a go buy ticket for Miami?

Lou I have to think of everything?

Lyla Tomorrow I going walk around all the hotel again.

Lou Why? You in need a exercise?

Lyla They might give me a waitressing job. Can't spend the rest a my life like this.

Lou Tonight, Lyla, we a go dress up, curl up we hair and go a dancehall.

Lyla I don't feel like dancing, Lou.

Lou You never feel like dancing till you step in a the dancehall and see all the sweet boys a pump and grind.

Lyla I'm not interested in boys, don't care how sweet they are.

Lou Poor little Lyla, don't be sad. Kenneth gone to a better place.

Lyla Don't be stupid, Lou. A better place. I want him here with me.

Lou I have a few dollars. Tonight me a go cook up some rice an' a little chicken. You can eat till you belly bust. (*She takes a card out of her pocket and reads it.*)

Lyla I thought you did throw that thing away.

Lou Bridie. Hyacinth Hotel. I wonder why she don't have a surname. A pop star?

Lyla Throw it away.

Lou We would be fool to throw it away, after she say she might have work for us.

Lyla I don't want to get mess up with the sorta work people from foreign have fe we. I never like how the woman a look pon me like me have something she want.

Lou How you mean? A want you think she want you? Woman like that nuh want yardie.

Lyla So why else you think them come a Jamaica? For the scenery?

Lou No harm in meeting the woman, Ly. At least we might get a drink outa it. The Hyacinth Hotel nice you know.

Lyla You go by youself. Me nah go nowhere.

Lou You would let me go to meet a strange woman in a hotel all on me own.

Lyla Is me fault if you too damn greedy?

Lou A nuh greedy, me greedy, Lyla? A curiosity. You nuh curious to find out what sorta work she going offer us?

Lyla A free drinks you a look.

Lou Might even get a night dinner outa it. Lobster, fry fish, desserts. An' she would pay for everything. You never see how she dress up? You never see how nice that woman look? How sweet she smell? Well then. If you nah come with me, me a go on me own.

Lyla You can't do that. I better come with you, keep you outa trouble.

Lou I did know say you would change you mind. Good.

SCENE FOUR

London. Waterloo Bridge.
   Allie, Pepper and Piglet enter. Piglet is restless. She continually walks up and down, looking around as if to make sure no one is watching them. She does this surreptitiously.

Pepper Don't the city look beautiful at midnight.

Piglet Now she's gone all romantic.

Pepper I could stand on this bridge all night and watch the sun come up, couldn't you?

Piglet She cries when you switch the lights on on the Christmas tree.

Pepper Shut up, Piglet.

Piglet My name isn't Piglet. It's Samantha.

Pepper Samantha? Where'd that come from, then?

Piglet It's my real name.

Pepper Samantha. I prefer Piglet. It suits her better, doesn't it?

   Allie doesn't reply to the question because she doesn't want to offend Piglet.

Allie You've been ever so kind to me today.

Pepper It's nothing, eh Piglet . . . Samantha, or whatever you call yourself. You'd do the same for us if we was strangers in your home town, wouldn't you? You looked so lonely when we saw you sitting there in that café. We could tell you was a stranger because you looked kind of frightened, looking up every time someone new walked in.

Allie I wasn't frightened. More curious.

Pepper I said to Piglet – didn't I, Piglet? – I said, bet she's new. I said, bet no one's even said hello to her since she got here, and I said to Piglet, I'm going to go up and say hello. I don't want her to think we're all stuck up and unfriendly, didn't I, Piglet?

Piglet Yeah.

Allie Thanks for the lunch and taking me around sight-seeing.

Pepper Didn't see many sights, did we? Alternative London we've shown you. The London you should see. All the little back streets and alleys. Low life, high life. There's people lived here all their lives haven't seen half of what you've seen.

Piglet Too happy sitting in their little houses, watching their little television sets.

Pepper What's that, Piglet?

Piglet We should start up as tour operators, coach rides to the other London.

Pepper There might be something in that you know, Piglet.

Piglet You got a boyfriend?

Pepper Piglet. You don't go around asking people things

like that. That's personal.

Allie No, no boyfriend. I travelled light, left everything back home except the clothes I stood up in.

Pepper It was a quick getaway, then?

Allie I wanted to get out as quickly as I could.

Pepper So are you planning on settling here or do you aim to go back home?

Allie I hadn't thought much about it. All I wanted was to get out.

Pepper I did the same. Long time ago now, though. I've been here ever since.

Piglet Have you got a job?

Allie Not yet. I'm looking.

Piglet Come on, Pepper, we haven't got all night. Let's get a move on.

Pepper So impetuous, our Samantha. I'm always trying to keep her in check. Calm down, Piglet, the night is young and you're wrong: we've got all the time in the world. You don't want to rush things.

Piglet What work did you do at home?

Allie Nothing, really. I was a shop assistant. Worked in the same shop since I was sixteen.

Piglet Anything legal considered.

Allie The most boring place on earth.

Pepper Boring is bad news for young girls. We make sure we do something interesting every day, don't we Piglet?

Allie I stuck it out for my mother, really. I didn't want to let her down.

Piglet Do you have a pink dress?

Pepper Piglet, what you asking her that for? That's a stupid question to ask her.

Piglet She looked like she might have a pink dress. With ribbons.

Pepper I think she's had a bit too much to drink, haven't you, Pig?

Allie I think I have too.

Pepper We can help you find a job, can't we Piglet? We got a few contacts round here who can help you out.

Allie I got a room. Now all I need is to get myself a regular job.

Pepper I said we'll help you. What else are friends for?

Allie I was so lucky to meet you both, wasn't I? I'm not afraid to say that I was beginning to get anxious about being here. This afternoon I was even beginning to contemplate going home again.

Pepper You don't want to do that.

Allie You wonder if there's any point if you don't know anybody.

Pepper And then things took a turn for the better and you met myself and my good friend Samantha over there. I'm telling you Piglet, you are no Samantha. Why don't you open them tins a Coke. I'm gasping. Thirsty, Allie?

Allie Not really. Must be all the excitement.

Pepper London is an exciting place, isn't it? The Coke, Piglet.

Piglet Which Coke?

Pepper In your hands.

Piglet Sorry, I thought you meant something else.

Pepper Oh, look at those birds.

While Pepper and Allie look at the birds, Piglet opens the can of Coke and puts something into it.

Allie My God, what's wrong with them?

Pepper It's the light from that lamp, see, shining on them.

Allie Doesn't it look as though they're a flock of little golden geese?

Pepper Bet you've never seen pigeons look so good, have you? Look at her face, Piglet, she looks just like a kid. I see, you've done the honours and cracked open our drinks. About time too, eh Allie? Our guest first, Pig.

Piglet My name is Samantha.

Pepper Since when? Since last Tuesday? You've always been Piglet. I like Piglet, so let's not hear any of that rubbish again, eh Pig?

Piglet gives Allie the drink.

Go on, you have a nice long drink of that. It'll make you feel good. It's like a tonic, isn't it?

Allie drinks.

That's what she is. A nice innocent little child, isn't she? And it's because of that that I've got to issue you with some advice. Trust nobody. You've got a good, kind nature and there's people will take advantage of that. You've got to toughen up, see. You don't want anybody to get one over on you, do you? And this place is notorious for that, I can tell you. Do you want to sit down, love?

Allie, looking a little weary, sits.

It has been a bit of a hard day, hasn't it?

Allie Trust nobody.

Pepper Always pretend to know where you're going even if you're lost. You can always stop and look properly when the danger's passed.

Piglet The best piece of advice, though, is to carry a fuckin' rubber cosh on you at all times.

Pepper Where did we get her from, eh? Shut up, Piglet.

Allie is very woozy at this point.

Allie The birds are on fire. It's a sign. A good sign. God, I'm so tired.

Pepper Why don't you lie down?

Allie lies down.

Allie I had to run away. Mum said that I was a bad lot and that I would never come to anything. I'm not a bad lot.

Pepper 'Course not.

Allie I'm a good girl.

Pepper That's obvious, ennit Pig?

Piglet Eh?

Allie And if anyone says different, I'll bash their fucking . . . (*She falls into a deep sleep.*)

Pepper Quick, Pig. Her wallet.

Piglet Not much in it.

Pepper Take whatever's there. Seems a shame in a way. Don't she look peaceful lying there?

Piglet We're too poor for pity.

Pepper You're right about that. And what was all that about 'call me Samantha'?

Piglet I just felt like being somebody different for a change.

Pepper Pink party dresses.

Piglet I hate pink. (*taking hold of Allie's hand*) This is a nice little ring.

Pepper Don't take that. It must have sentimental value.

Piglet I want it. You never let me have anything nice.

Pepper We do have some conscience, don't we Pig?

Piglet I've always wanted a ring like that.

Pepper Take it then, and don't say I never give you nothing.

Piglet We leaving her here?

Pepper What else we gonna do with her? Take her with us? What for?

Piglet Can we leave her here? It's freezing cold.

Pepper Since when did you acquire compassion? I'm never going to call you Samantha again. Come on, let's go before she wakes up.

Piglet She ain't gonna wake up for ages. I put enough in there.

Pepper She'll wake up thinking she's died and gone to heaven, won't she?

Piglet She may just freeze to death.

Pepper Come on, let's go. (*Throws the empty wallet at Piglet.*) Next time you choose a new name why don't you choose something meaningful like Rebecca or Ruth?

Piglet I don't feel like a Rebecca or Ruth.

Piglet and Pepper leave.

Jamaica.
Hotel bar. Lou has had too much to drink. Lyla has drunk quite a lot too, but isn't giving in to tipsiness in the same way as Lou. Bridie is sober.

Lou (*laughing*) She run us outa she back yard. You know like the way you shoo chicken? Tha's how she shoo us outa she back yard. You shoulda see us. I never run so fast in me life.

Bridie (*laughing*) I can just imagine.

Lou She say, 'you try to thief me melon again, me a go set me dog pon you'. An' we a look pon each other because we know say she nuh have a dog. Anyway, two week later we walk past she yard an' we see a sign on her gate say 'Guard dog' an' a picture of something look like wolf. So I say to Lyla, I have to see this wolf dog for meself. So me climb up over the wall and, Lord God, if she haven't got a wolf dog a stand guard over she melon. But you know something? That guard dog skinny like a skeleton. She so mean, she nah feed it. Dog look up at me as if it a beg me to climb over the wall and save it. One time . . .

Lyla I sure she don't want to hear any more about Mrs Campbell meagre dog.

Bridie Come on, tell me. Beats listening to these men talking business all evening.

Lyla Why don't we talk about you?

23

Bridie I've spent all morning talking about myself. I'd rather hear your stories.

Lou So many funny things happen in that neighbourhood. Like the time old mother Ellis frighten off gunman.

Lyla Why she want to hear about mother Ellis?

Lou Shut up Lyla, you can't see I'm talking to the woman.

Lyla Talk too much. I don't like you making fun of my neighbourhood.

Bridie She doesn't mean any harm. She's not laughing at anybody. She talks about it because she loves it.

Lou Shut up and let me talk, Lyla.

Lyla She drunk as hell.

Lou You don't like to see me having a good time, ennit? She can be such a sour sap sometimes, you know. Tha's what them should call you sour sap.

Lyla And what they would call you, Lou? Loose lip Lou.

Lou Miss Ellis must be – what? – eighty years old now. Hair white off. Bow leg. Can hardly walk without stop every two step to catch her breath. Like this. Gunman call a Miss Ellis yard a look for some boy. You should a hear the noise. Miss Ellis run outa her house a scream blue murder. Gunman frighten. Them must think them a raise duppy or something. Them run outa Miss Ellis house a scream out in fear with Miss Ellis chasing behind them with a foot a shoe a lick them in them head and shout like a tornado. You remember that, Lyla?

Bridie (*laughing*) I can just see that now. A little old lady running out of her house, chasing these great macho gunmen.

Lyla Why don't you tell her how them come back two day later and how them find what them was looking for?

Lou You want to spoil up me fun or something, Lyla? All this talk about blood and killing.

Lyla You hear me say anything about killing?

Lou You get some laugh in the community, but is hard too, you know. Me and Lyla was hoping that if we start up a little business that we could get a little money together, save up enough to buy a little house outside the community.

Lyla Why you don't just go and tell her all you little day-dream. (*to Bridie*) One day we going be so rich we going buy a house in Beverly Hills.

Bridie In the US?

Lou Kingston. Is just a dream.

Lyla Is just a joke.

Bridie It might feel like that right now, perhaps, but you never know what'll happen in the future, do you?

Lyla We know all right.

Lou The business not doing well at all.

Lyla You know a lot about us. Why you don't tell us about yourself?

Bridie What is there to tell?

Lyla You in Jamaica for work or pleasure?

Bridie Like everybody else in this hotel, I'm here on business.

Lyla What business you in?

Bridie Same as everybody else: buying and selling.

Lyla Taking advantage of the free zone?

Bridie Of course. Why not?

Lyla Everybody taking advantage of the free zone. Come to Jamaica, beautiful beaches and very cheap labour.

Lou Our auntie work in a factory making T-shirt and, you know, she could never buy one a them T-shirt herself because it would cost a week wages.

Bridie I hate that. I believe in paying people what they're worth.

Lou I like you suit.

Bridie I travel so much that I've adopted a very practical attitude towards clothes.

Lou You travel a lot?

Bridie All over the world. The States, Europe – Spain, France, Britain, Amsterdam. All over the world.

Lou I would like to travel.

Lyla Dream on, Lou.

Lou Them shoes nice too.

Bridie Italian. Though I've never been to Italy. I bought these in London.

Lou America, Englan'. I would like to see those places.

Bridie You might yet.

Lou Never. I will never get outa here.

Bridie With that attitude, I've no doubt you won't. You've got to start believing in yourself.

Lou What's the use in believing in meself? Even if I did there wouldn't be any work for me. You could go mad if you had too much faith in yourself.

Bridie What I'm saying is that opportunity follows faith.

Lyla You mean we make our own luck? Just like all those boys who get kill by gunman. They had a lot a faith in themself.

Bridie Perhaps it was the wrong kind of faith.

Lou You always stay in hotel like this?

Bridie I travel so much I don't have a proper home.

Lyla Is there a wrong kind of faith?

Bridie Every time I come here I'm amazed at the amount of talent that's going to waste. If you could only tap that . . .

Lou Nobody care if you starve.

Lyla We get by all right.

Bridie I'll bet you two are good hard workers given half a chance.

Lou I ain't had a proper job for years.

Bridie And I'm willing to put my money where my mouth is. How do you two fancy earning a little cash?

Lou You giving us a job?

Bridie I'm bored of sitting round the hotel bar all night. I'd love to go to a club. Have some fun, for God's sake. You two could be my guides. I'll bet you know some good places.

Lyla We don't go round the clubs. We got better things to do.

Lou Come on, Ly, we know a lot a good clubs. There's the Gemini, the Tropicana, the Yellow Orchid.

Lyla I have a feeling she don't want to go to clubs where tourist go, do you?

Bridie No. No tourist clubs.

Lyla She want to go to places where we would go by weself.

Bridie That's right.

Lou But we always go to the tourist clubs. It's safer.

Bridie Oh, come on. Let's have a good time. A few drinks, dancing, dinner if you want to. I hate being a tourist.

Lou We got to go home now, ennit Ly?

Lyla No we don't, Lou. She want to see Kingston. Come on, let's show her Kingston.

SCENE SIX

London. Street.
Allie sits on the ground. Olu enters. Allie covers her face with an item of clothing. A coin is tossed on-stage. Olu picks it up.

Allie Please Miss, spare some change for a cup a tea.

Olu stands and watches Allie.

Please Miss, just a few coppers.

Olu Do I look as though I have spare change?

Allie Please. I have nothing.

Olu What makes you think that even if I could, that I would give my hard-earned cash to you?

Allie I was mugged. My landlady chucked me out of her

house because I couldn't afford the rent. I'm all alone in the city. I haven't eaten for two weeks. I'm not very good at begging.

Olu And is that my fault? By the look of you, you are strong and healthy. Why don't you look for a job? The rest of us have to work very hard for our money. Do you think that we're going to squander it away on people like you? You make me sick. (*She starts to walk away.*)

Allie Please. I used to be just like you, had a job, family. My skin was soft just like yours.

Olu Look, I'd like to help you, but I have nothing myself. All I have are a few coppers. Even if I was to give you something, just think how bad that would be for both of us. You would feel humiliated and I would get caught up in the superiority of being the one who gave. We would both lose out. Listen, the best way I can help you is to let you find a way out of your problem by yourself. Believe me, in the long run this is the best way.

Olu starts to go. Allie calls after her.

Allie Thank you for your kindness.

Olu Don't demean yourself with thanks. I don't deserve them. (*She leaves.*)

SCENE SEVEN

Jamaica.
Bridie, Lyla and Lou.
Lyla and Lou are struggling with something that they each hold up under their skirts. We cannot see what they are doing. Bridie watches them. One of the girls, Lyla, is obviously finding the whole exercise extremely painful. Lou is having an easier time of it.

Bridie On the plane, I don't want you to even look at one another, not even a glance. I'd have got you separate flights if that had been possible, but as it is I'm going to have to rely on your self-control. You got your money?

Lou Yes, Miss Thompson.

Bridie When you get out of the airport, I want each of you to take a taxi straight to the hotel. Johnny will be in touch with you. We've booked you into a nice hotel in London and while you're waiting you can have anything you want – order room service and put it on the bill.

Lou Thank you, Miss Thompson.

Lyla cries out.

Bridie Lubricant. You need to use a lot more lubricant. I'll be arriving in London the day after you. I'll give you the rest of your money and make sure you get back on the plane safely.

Lyla cries out.

Lyla I can't do this, Miss Thompson. It hurts.

Bridie Of course you can do it. Look at your sister. She managed.

Lyla How can I walk with that inside me?

Bridie Perhaps you're just not ready for this.

Lou She jus' nervous, Miss Thompson.

Bridie What you need to do is to relax. You need some privacy. Why don't you go into the bathroom?

Lyla All right, Miss Thompson.

Bridie Just take your time. You don't have to be at the airport for another three hours.

Lyla I'm sorry, Miss Thompson. (*She leaves the room.*)

Bridie Of all the girls just waiting to do this job, all those girls desperate for work in the ghetto . . .

Lou looks at Bridie beseechingly.

I know, she's nervous and her body's shut down.

Lou She will be all right, Miss Thompson. None of us ever done anything like this before.

Bridie I was worried about using sisters as it was. You may find it difficult to resist talking to each other on the plane.

Lou She look at me, I won't take any notice.

Bridie You've got what it takes. It's baby sister I'm worried about. Perhaps I should send you through alone.

Lou This is the first chance we've had. There's nuttin' in Trenchtown for us. I won't go without her, Miss Thompson.

Bridie As an only child I can't say that I've ever understood the bond between sisters.

Lou All we have is each other. We have a mother but she sleep naked a roadside. Sometime I see her I have to turn my head away like as if I don't know her.

Pause. Bridie gets up.

Bridie Listen, Lou, I know what it's like to have no one, nothing. We come from the same place. I grew up in Trenchtown too.

Lou You from the ghetto, Miss Thompson?

Bridie Surprised?

Lou I thought you was American.

31

Bridie The accent started as an affectation when I was a child and later became part of my character. As for the ghetto . . . it isn't ingrained, you know. You can wash it off.

Lou I would never a believe you was from Trenchtown.

Bridie Of course I've since been to the States several times.

Lou That's somewhere I would love to visit.

Bridie Well, why don't we plan a little trip for you?

Lou To the States?

Bridie Why not? You do good on this job and we'll see what we can do.

Lou I can't believe it.

Bridie It was my dream too. (*Slight pause. She looks at Lou.*) You are so like me.

Lou Me?

Bridie When I was your age. You're intelligent – you don't miss a trick, do you?

Lou People tell me I'm too sharp.

Bridie If I was to find fault with you, I would say that you're too trusting. You'll learn, though. Take my advice, trust no one. Not even that baby sister of yours.

Lou Lyla? What would Lyla do to me?

Bridie Take no notice of me. I'm just a cynical old hag.

Lou If I couldn't trust Lyla, then who could I trust?

Bridie All I'm saying is that you don't want anybody to hold you back. I can see you've got a future. You could end up going all over the world.

Lou All over the world.

Lyla enters, unseen.

Bridie Anybody else looking at you doesn't see what I see. I see someone with endless potential. I want you to think of me as . . . well, as a big sister. If there's anything you need, anything bothering you, just come to me and I'll see what I can do. OK?

Lou All right, Miss Thompson.

Bridie Now, we'd better make sure you're all ready to go. All packed?

Lou Yes, Miss Thompson.

Bridie Tickets and passports?

Lou I got everything in this wallet here.

Bridie You look fantastic. That dress suits you.

Lou Thank you Miss Thompson.

Bridie Call me Bridie.

Lou Thank you Bridie.

Bridie I'll take you shopping in London. Like that?

Lyla I finish, Miss Thompson.

Bridie Great. You feeling all right?

Lyla Yes, thank you.

Bridie There. I told you all you had to do was relax, didn't I? Come on, I'll take you both to lunch before I drive you to the airport. I'll just go downstairs and settle my bill.

Bridie leaves the room. Lou looks at Lyla and smiles excitedly. Lyla doesn't smile back.

Lyla It didn't hurt you, putting that thing inside you?

Lou Of course it hurt me. (*Slight pause.*) Bridie taking us shopping in London.

Lyla She nuh like me.

Lou She like us, man.

Lyla Is you she like. She nah give me any more work after this.

Lou Then me a tell her that me nah go without you.

Lyla I don't know if I want this kind a work anyway.

Lou You joking? Fly a England? Luxury Hotel? You want to go back to Trenchtown?

Lyla Nuttin' wrong wi' Trenchtown.

Lou Step outside you door, you nuh know if is going to be police or gunman war. Leave you man in bed asleep, come back find him sleeping in the arms a Jesus.

Lyla Stop it Lou.

Lou Kenneth woulda glad say you picking up on you feet again.

Lyla Kenneth was a Christian.

Lou That never stop him getting involve wit Don, did it? Now, pick up you passport and don't forget you ticket.

Lyla I not going, Lou. I can't. (*She takes the coke-filled condom out of her handbag.*)

Lou How you mean? Bridie got everything plan.

Lyla I may come outa the ghetto but I have respect for my body. I not some kinda carrier bag.

Lou I want to go to England, Paris. How else I going to

America?

Lyla What if they catch you?

Lou We got to live, Ly. Look how Harriet go to Columbia come back dress up in Gucci and Gabbana.

Lyla An' how she come back dress up the last time we see her? In a wooden one-piece.

Lou You ain't got no ambition. You ain't cut out for this sorta work. Why don't you get back to Trenchtown. (*Slight pause. Lyla reacts.*) We nuh Siamese twin. Why you can't let me go?

Lyla picks up her suitcase but doesn't move. Bridie re-enters.

Bridie Lunch. Come on, let's go. Is everything all right?

Lou Yes. I'm coming.

Bridie Good, because we don't want to be late. Hours yet, I know, but I'm obsessive about time.

Bridie and Lou go to the door. Lou exits. Lyla stands in the middle of the room. Bridie looks back at her.

Bridie Lyla?

Lyla (*after a brief pause*) Coming. (*She leaves the room with Bridie.*)

SCENE EIGHT

London.
Allie lies in the street. Gradually she comes to. A little groggy. Looking around herself as if trying to make sense of what she has woken up to. Two 'bad girls' emerge from the darkness.

Bad Girl 1 Pretty girl in the dark.

Bad Girl 2 Mascara's run.

Bad Girl 1 Frightful.

Bad Girl 2 Mother never tell you it wasn't safe to walk the streets this time a night?

Bad Girl 1 That's when all the creatures come out to play.

Bad Girl 2 We can't bear to face the daylight.

Allie Leave me alone. (*She scrambles away.*)

Bad Girl 1 Only thing that separates us from the animals is the ability to walk upright.

Bad Girl 2 That and the power of speech.

Bad Girl 1 Not to mention that of thought.

Bad Girl 2 And emotion.

Bad Girl 1 Now that's debatable.

Bad Girl 2 What is?

Bad Girl 1 The ability of animals to feel pain.

Bad Girl 2 I have it on good authority that this is privileged to the homosapien and even more privileged to the female of the species.

Bad Girl 1 Debatable.

Bad Girl 2 What is?

Bad Girl 1 Whether men and women are part of the same species or whether women are a subspecies within the main species.

Bad Girl 2 Don't be daft.

Bad Girl 1 Main species homo-caucasian with hetero-erotic tendencies. Everything else is baloney.

Bad Girl 2 Everything else?

Bad Girl 1 Women, criminals, blacks and children.

Bad Girl 2 Don't be so bloody stupid. (*to Allie*) Say anything, her, for the sake of an argument, even if she has to make it up.

Bad Girl 1 Had that on good authority. Read it in a book.

Bad Girl 2 (*to Allie*) See. She can't read.

Bad Girl 1 You'd better get inside quick, before it strikes midnight.

Bad Girl 2 You look like the sort of woman what should be indoors at this time a night.

Bad Girl 1 A lady.

Bad Girl 2 No one could accuse us of being a lady.

Bad Girl 1 Too right they couldn't.

Bad Girl 2 We cruise the streets at night, sometimes glimpsing the world behind the net curtains.

Bad Girl 1 The cosy glow of a middle-class fireplace.

Bad Girl 2 Children's toys strewn over the living-room carpet.

Bad Girl 1 We're the girls who creep into your house while you're asleep.

Bad Girl 2 Bad girls.

Bad Girl 1 We sit in your kitchen drinking cups of coffee and eating chocolate biscuits.

Bad Girl 2 Go through your wardrobe right under your nose.

Bad Girl 1 Breast-feed your babies, then dandle them on our knees to send them back to sleep.

Bad Girl 2 Prick holes in your marital condoms.

Bad Girl 1 Spit in your contact lens cleaner fluid.

Bad Girl 2 Fuck your husband in his sleep like he's never been fucked before, so he wakes in the morning bruised and tantalized.

Bad Girl 1 If we feel like it, we cover our traces so well you'll never know we've been.

Bad Girl 2 Until you look for that coral necklace he gave you for your thirtieth birthday only to find you've misplaced it.

Bad Girl 1 Or just for the fuck of it, we'll create havoc: spill all the milk, break all the bottles.

Bad Girl 2 Piss on your Habitat settee.

Allie I'm not scared of you.

Bad Girl 1 No?

Bad Girl 2 (*quickly grabs Allie, pulls out knife which she holds to Allie's throat*) You fucking should be. Give us all your money.

Allie Handbag. Over there.

Bad Girl 1 retrieves the handbag while Bad Girl 2 continues to hold Allie by the throat. She takes out the purse. There's nothing in it.

Bad Girl 1 Not even fag money.

Bad Girl 2 What about credit cards?

Bad Girl 1 (*searching the wallet*) The cupboard was bare. No wonder she's walking the streets.

Bad Girl 2 (*letting Allie go*) Thought you might have had a few bob.

Allie Why? What makes you think I'm any different to you?

Bad Girl 2 Fur coat and no knickers.

Allie Give me back my handbag.

Bad Girl 1 You want it, come and get it.

Allie walks over to Bad Girl 1 and reaches for the handbag which Bad Girl 1 pulls away from her. She taunts Allie like this and Allie begins to lose her temper. Allie grabs Bad Girl 1 and pushes her to the ground. Bad Girl 2 watches amused as they fight silently, not seemingly making any progress, i.e., there is no winner; one minute one of them seems to have the upper hand and this is then upset when it is gained by the other.

Bad Girl 2 I could make a killing out of this if I charged the dirty mac brigade. I think I might be on to something there.

Allie You fight dirty.

Bad Girl 1 Pull your hair out the fucking roots.

Allie It's a weave.

Bad Girl 1 (*on top*) Even better. There's more than one way to skin a cat.

Bad Girl 2 Bit a mud, flimsy costumes, nothing vulgar, mind.

Allie, on top, grabs hold of Bad Girl 1's neck and squeezes it.

39

Bad Girl 1 I'm not playing any more. You're hurting me.

Bad Girl 2 Steady on. You're hurting her. You're not playing fair, breaking the rules, Marquess of Queensberry and all that.

While Bad Girl 2 speaks, Bad Girl 1 is struggling to free herself from Allie who squeezes her neck even tighter. Bad Girl 1 gasps and we see her reach out her hand as though trying to grab hold of something. The hand trembles and then flops down onto the ground. Pause.

You bitch. You've bloody killed her.

Allie gets up slowly.

Don't you dare come near me, you murderer. I got this knife.

Allie walks toward her, fearless, and removes the knife while Bad Girl 2 stares at her like a frightened rabbit, then backs away. Allie follows her.

Allie I've had enough, right, of you, me mum, the whole bloody lot of you. I been fucked over once too many times.

Bad Girl 2 What you gonna do to me, you monster?

Allie And him. Every time Mum went out the room he'd touch me with his stinking fingers, hold my face, make me look at him. Then I'd do my disappearing trick, will myself to disappear. My body, just a body. (*to Bad Girl 2*) Get over there, quick.

Bad Girl 2 You touch me I only got to whistle and my mates'll all come out of the darkness. There's about ten of 'em. A gang. They're watching us now. You lay a finger on me and you're dead. You're lucky that they've thought to turn a blind eye to your little murder there . . . All I got to do is whistle.

Allie brandishes the knife and Bad Girl 2 turns on her heels and runs off-stage. Bad Girl 1 sits up, rubbing her eyes.

Bad Girl 1 Where am I?

Allie brandishes her knife.

Oh God, I remember. All right. All right. I'm going.

Bad Girl 1 gets up shakily, brushes herself down and leaves the stage with as much dignity as she can muster.

Allie (*heavily out of breath as she retrieves her handbag and other personal effects*) My God, what's happening to me? Fighting in the street like a fishwife. I feel . . . I feel . . . (*Standing, trying to catch her breath.*) I feel fucking brilliant.

Bridie enters. She throws a coin to Allie who catches it. As she speaks she throws more coins to her. By the end of her speech she is throwing coins to the ground and Allie is scrambling around on all fours to collect them up.

Bridie Begging is the purest form of commercialism. Certainly it's the most honest, apart, that is, from the beggar's promise to the beneficent passer-by to buy herself a cup of tea. I guess that this is a necessary lie. Imagine if you said, 'I'm saving up to buy some crack cocaine or a bottle of meths', then that would send the donor into a right old pickle, wouldn't it? In giving you money, she is giving you life, can she be seen to condone death? The Samaritan who gives to a beggar would, if these were the Dark Ages, be buying herself a place in Heaven. Nothing's changed. You have, when giving, to repress the inevitable sensation of superiority. After all, this is a transaction just like any other and what the passer-by is purchasing from the beggar is an unseen lucky charm to ward against the same fate befalling her.

Allie Thank you very much, miss. You're very kind. It's a miracle.

Bridie What is?

Allie You appearing like that, just as I was completely down on my luck.

Bridie You think it's fate? How about if I buy you breakfast? You look as though you could murder some toast.

Allie You're very kind.

Bridie Oh, don't worry. I don't expect you to supplicate yourself. Besides, you will be paying for it. Eventually.

Act Two

SCENE NINE

Bridie pretends to 'die' on stage. She clutches at her stomach. It is very melodramatic. After a few mock spasms, she lies still for a long while and then sits up.

Bridie Remember that game winking murder that we played as children? You choose a detective and send them out of the room. Then you choose a murderer. The murderer has to kill everyone by winking at them when the detective isn't looking. The detective has to guess whodunnit before everybody gets killed. The real fun of the game is the surprise of death because you have to die in the most melodramatic and obvious way possible. There is no form of death that I haven't seen. Murder by gun, suffocation and stabbing. ODs from burst condoms are the most graphic.

Light up on Olu on-stage, holding her stomach.

One minute you're going through customs happy as Larry, the next minute, well . . .

Olu collapses, enacting what Bridie describes.

First you start to gasp for breath because the drug enters the blood stream and deprives you of oxygen. Then the body goes into spasms, as though you were having an epileptic fit. You'll cry out, but there will be no words because you'll have lost the facility for words. Nothing but an agonized screaming. The whole thing lasts several minutes. It's the quickest death ever.

Olu is dead. Bridie covers her with a sheet.

Live like a mule, die like a mule.

Allie and Bridie in a London hotel room. As she speaks,
Allie removes small packets of coke from her person. She
takes off a wig she wears in which drugs have been
secreted and peels wide strips of plaster from her legs and
her waist under which, again, there are packets of drugs.
She talks excitedly.

Allie All through the flight I wanted to scratch my head,
but I didn't want to draw attention to my hair. Besides,
what if I scratched my head and the wig moved then
everybody would have known I was wearing a wig,
wouldn't they? They might get suspicious. So I had to put
up with this itch. It drove me mad. I tried everything: I
tried to ignore it, but the more you try to ignore something the more you think about it, don't you? So the itch
is starting to get worse and worse and I'm trying to find
ways to get rid of it without actually touching it. I try to
go to sleep but the itch won't let me. I try to get myself so
drunk that I'll fade away in an alcoholic blur, but the
drink and the flight simply stimulate me and the itch is
getting more ticklish. To make matters worse, I develop
an itch on my stomach, so now I'm getting itchy all over
and I can't do anything about it because I don't want to
make the air hostesses suspect anything, and I can't go to
the loo as this enormous bloke in the seat beside me has
fallen asleep and I don't want to wake him up.

Bridie (*completing her counting of the packets*) You did a
great job.

Allie So I just had to exercise self-control and grin and
bear it.

Bridie Not a bad thing to have to learn.

Allie I wanted to scratch myself raw, but soon as I got

out of the airport, the itch just disappeared.

Bridie Just goes to show, doesn't it? Nerves takes us all in strange ways.

Allie Do you think that's what it was?

Bridie One girl who worked for me had to spend an hour being sick in the bathroom. Another girl came out in big red lumps all over her face.

Allie Going through customs was another matter altogether. My heart was thumping. I could swear that everybody was staring at me. I noticed this man at customs looking at me. Should I look back at him, should I drop my gaze or should I smile?

Bridie Never smile. A smile is submissive. You want to be in control.

Allie Then, somehow, I don't know how, it was like somebody else took over. This really cool woman who had no nerves. My heart stopped beating, there was this silence inside me. I felt full of this power and I just walked past customs as though I expected to be allowed straight through. And I was.

Bridie You seemed cool as a cucumber when I picked you up. Very cool for a first timer.

Allie I can't describe the high, Bridie. I felt like I could do anything I wanted. Jump through flaming hoops, race with panthers. Nothing's ever felt as good. Then it all come back to me, every single official at that airport had somebody else's face.

Bridie What do you mean 'somebody else's face'?

Allie Every face that's ever scowled at me, looked down at me, denied me. Headmasters, teachers, shop assistants, petty officials. I walked through customs sticking two fingers up at them all and they couldn't do a thing about it. One–nil to me.

Bridie I'll take you out for a meal to celebrate.

Allie I'm starving, but I'm too excited to eat.

Bridie You're still on a high. Come here. (*She pulls Allie down and starts to massage her back.*) Calm down. It's all there for you, waiting for you.

Allie My stomach's still turning somersaults. When are you going to use me again?

Bridie There's no hurry, no rush at all. We don't want you burning out.

Allie I feel like I can take on the world. One day I'll be like you: sit back, take things easy and let someone else do all the hard work.

Bridie (*reacting to what Allie has said, but not letting it show*) Most people have this problem with coming down. Perhaps this might help you get your feet back on the ground. (*She hands Allie an envelope.*)

Allie I was beginning to lose my self-respect.

Bridie We all want to be able to stand on our own two feet, don't we? Who wants hand-outs and pity?

Allie Now I can feel it building itself up again. That woman – the cool one, the one with no nerves – is gone. Maybe she was just a fantasy. She was icy clean and six foot. She's melted now and it's just me, but I can feel myself getting strong.

Bridie You don't know how strong you could be. You did a good job, Allie, but there is one thing.

Allie What?

Bridie Make-up.

Allie Make-up?

Bridie You wore too much.

Allie I only put on a bit of lipstick and mascara.

Bridie It was the first thing I thought when I saw you: 'she's got far too much warpaint on'. You don't need to hide behind that kind of mask. Dressing up the way you did, you draw attention to yourself.

Allie I'm sorry, Bridie.

Bridie It's OK.

Allie I've messed up, haven't I?

Bridie After having got through with all this? I should think not.

Allie Because I want to be good.

Bridie Don't we all? It's the female condition.

Allie I don't want you to think that I'm a silly little girl. I want to work for you.

Bridie Of course I want you to work for me again. All you need is a little fine tuning. I've been in this game for over fifteen years. I know what I'm talking about. I'll never bullshit you. I'll be more honest with you than your own mother.

Allie My mother wasn't honest.

Bridie No?

Allie When my dad left she said it would always be just me and her and then she took in the first man who showed an interest in her.

Bridie Some women just can't live without a man, can they?

47

Allie He was a creep, crept all over the house at night and all over me, fucking bastard.

Bridie And that's why you ran away.

Allie Would you stay? How could I? He smelt of beer, fags and piss. I can still smell him.

Bridie My mother abandoned me when I was a child. I've been fending for myself since I was fourteen years old.

Allie I missed her at first, but she chose him over me and now I think that she deserves him.

Bridie And now you've got a new life, just like I had to find for myself. I won't lie to you, Allie, this life can sometimes be very tough, but you'll always know where you stand. You will never be betrayed.

SCENE ELEVEN

London.
  Bridie entertains her colleagues, Sammie and Rog.

Rog I play this little game. I look around the shop, all shifty like, as though I'm not aware that they're watching me and I pick out the most expensive items and disappear into the changing room. While I'm in there the shop assistant keeps surprising me in me underwear to ask if I'm all right and I come out to find her wearing a patronizing smile and holding out her arms for clothes she's sure I can't afford. This is the best bit. I sail right past her, put the clothes down on the counter and take out my American Express gold card. Funny how the little credit card machines always break down when I go near them. Must be the effect I have on machinery. They've got to have some other proof of identity. Have I got anything other than a gas bill? Something with my signature on it?

48

Something other than a driver's licence? Something with my picture on it? A passport? Immediately the credit card machine starts working again and they're all over me, apologizing for having caused me any inconvenience.

Sammie You are so bitter, Rog.

Rog I rose above their petty bigotry.

Sammie Rising above it would mean not giving a toss about what they thought of you. After all, you were the one with the credit card.

Bridie enters.

Bridie Get stuck in girls, why don't you. You should know by now that I don't stand on ceremony.

Rog I was telling Sammie about my last shopping spree.

Bridie I'd have thought you had enough clothes.

Rog I like clothes.

Sammie You must have whole rooms in your house just full of clobber.

Rog I like shopping. Doesn't everybody?

Bridie Sammie spends all her money on original works of art. Please girls, you're making me nervous not eating.

Rog She always wants to see us stuffing our gobs, have you noticed?

Sammie You got to say this for her though, she always lays on a good spread.

Bridie Courtesy of the hotel. I haven't cooked since 1980.

Rog I still don't understand why you sold that beautiful house to go and live out of a suitcase again.

Bridie I just couldn't settle, Rog. I felt stuck. At least in a

49

hotel you always feel as if you're going somewhere. En route. It's like running on a treadmill. When you come off it you still feel as though you're moving. When I stop travelling, I still feel like I'm flying. I suppose if I settled down I'd have to establish some sort of relationship with myself. I can't say I particularly want to. Does that make me shallow?

Sammie I couldn't live for work the way that you do.

Bridie I've got the best job in the world.

Rog Do you ever want to leave it all behind, settle down?

Bridie Never.

Sammie I want to propose a toast.

Rog What are we celebrating?

Sammie To all the prodigal daughters licking their lips on fatted calf, to all the lost little lambkins come to their senses and returned to the fold. To Sabrina.

Rog Sabrina? Why we toasting that little cow?

Bridie Didn't we tell you, Rog? We found her.

Rog You found her?

Bridie It wasn't difficult.

Sammie She was lost without my guidance, didn't know what to do with herself.

Bridie She had nowhere to go but home.

Sammie Started spending money like a lottery winner.

Bridie It's awful when they start to get cocky.

Sammie When we found her she was like a fly that had fallen in a glass of wine: fat and drunk on her own greed.

Bridie Our little Sabrina turns out to be a junkie.

Sammie I'd never have taken her on if I'd known. I'm usually very good at spotting that sort of thing.

Rog You could almost feel sorry for her, couldn't you?

Bridie We took her to see Cliveden. Not many girls get to meet Cliveden.

Sammie You ever been to Cliveden's house, Rog? It's all classical music and antiques.

Bridie I must say he handled her very well. He can be quite fatherly when he wants to be. He's talking to her really gently, telling her he's not angry with her, he understands why she did it. Says he even admires her initiative. Then she spills everything like she's on an analyst's couch and her sob story is spilling out of her. And he's just sitting there nodding and smiling, his head cocked to the side like a kindly uncle. Then all of a sudden he gets up and goes to his desk and he tells her that he forgives her, that he wants her to work for him again but that this time they've got to draw up a proper contract with each other. He opens a drawer and pulls out this contract.

Sammie Only it's not a bloody contract, it's a bloody gun.

Bridie He takes it out and points it at her head. He makes her get down on her knees . . . on her knees and he tells her exactly what's going down and makes her agree to his terms. You can barely hear what she's saying. Anyway, he puts the gun away and tells her to get up. She refuses. And then we realize why.

Sammie She's only gone and pissed on his Axminster. (*She laughs.*)

Bridie You know how mean he is. He'll have to have the damn thing cleaned now.

Sammie I gave her Brownie points for that.

Bridie and Sammie are laughing. Rog is silent.

Bridie He was only trying to scare her. We'd never have let him hurt her, you know that.

Rog I'd a pissed me'self an' all if someone held a gun to my head.

Bridie It was just a joke.

Rog Some joke.

Sammie Come on, Rog, don't be such an old stick in the mud.

Rog I don't quite get Cliveden's sense of humour.

Bridie Come on, girls, don't stand on ceremony. We're not working now. Kick off your shoes. It's not often we get to enjoy ourselves, is it? (*She hands round drinks.*)

Sammie Whatever happened to your ghost, Bridie?

Bridie Oh that.

Sammie Did that priest get rid of it?

Bridie He reckons she's a dispossessed soul broken loose of purgatory or something. There was nothing he could do.

Sammie So you've got to put up with it following you around for ever.

Rog Some poor dead girl. Why'd she choose you?

Bridie My maternal instincts? Who knows? I want to propose another toast.

Sammie Can you hear her now, Bridie?

Bridie Oh, what does it matter?

Rog What's she saying?

Bridie Come on, a toast.

Rog You ask me, that's a fucking life sentence.

Bridie Oh, I don't know. It could be worse. I'll just have to learn to live with it, won't I?

SCENE TWELVE

Allie and Lou have been locked up in a police cell.

Allie What do you think'll happen to us?

Lou Bridie tell me that anything happen, she will be straight here to help me out. She going to get the best lawyers. The people she work for very high up, you know. This not some little diggy-diggy operation. They got all sort a high up people working for them: airline official, custom officer, judge.

Allie I've never been to prison.

Lou I'm not frightened. They can't touch us.

Allie I noticed you at Kingston airport. I just happened to stand behind you when you was checking in. If we hadn't ended up in here I wouldn't have given you a second thought. Funny how fate is, ennit?

Lou I had all my things with me, all my shopping. My new suit and a shoulder bag. Pray God they don't thief these things from me. (*calling out*) You better not take my things, you thiefing wretch unno. You better give them back to me otherwise . . .

Allie (*calling*) I want to make a phone call.

Lou I did leave a message for Bridie at the hotel.

Allie Imagine, she must have been dashing between our rooms like in a farce.

Lou I want to make a phone call. I didn't get through the first time.

Allie You left a message though?

Lou I didn't talk to Bridie.

Allie If you left a message, they won't allow you to make another call. We've both lost all our lives.

Lou I'm not frightened.

Allie Everybody's frightened of going to prison.

Lou I'm not going to prison.

Allie They always said that that's how I'd end up. I couldn't understand why they said that.

Lou You talk too much.

Allie I hate being locked up. They used to lock me into my bedroom.

Lou I don't want to talk any more.

Slight pause.

Allie Round about now Bridie will be boarding the plane.

Lou She going to cancel her flight.

Allie The stewardess is showing her to her seat. She's put her luggage away and clicked on the safety belt. She's reading the complimentary in-flight magazine, poring over glossy adverts and gadgets. She likes toys. She's thinking that she must buy herself one a them electronic organizers and wonders why she doesn't have one already. She's slipped her shoes off. In a minute she'll accept a complimentary drink and nod off to sleep.

Lou You don't know what you're talking about. If she leave is because she have to, but she will come back as soon as she can.

Allie You're going to prison and Bridie won't give a fuck. (*calling*) I want to make a formal complaint. (*to Lou*) I'm sure that bitch enjoyed sticking her fingers up me. Did they search you? All my life I've been somebody that nobody noticed. I could always count on being the one they served last at a bar. People just wouldn't see me and now, all of a sudden, I'm standing out like a sore thumb, being dragged off for body searches.

Lou You see, I'm not you usual courier. I'm a professional. Working for meself more or less. I'm not one of them little girl: 'Oh, I love me boyfriend so much and he asked me to carry a package back for him and I guessed there might be something funny in it but – oh, I love him and I didn't want to lose him . . .'

Allie Bridie taught me how to put them in. Like a big sister teaching you how to use tampons.

Lou I have a future. A house, a car, nice clothes. I'm going to be in charge a me own life. Even back home I don't let anybody boss me around. I'm not scared a anybody. Not even gunman. You want shoot me, shoot me. I'm going to walk around with my head high. I tell you this, whatever happen I'm not going back to the ghetto. I'm going to get my life together. They think they can treat me any way and any how. I'm going to be somebody. I ain't no fucking mule.

SCENE THIRTEEN

A prison cell. Lou and Allie. Lou lies on her bed curled up into a ball.

55

Allie Donna gives me this love letter for Alice, right, but she doesn't tell me Letitia's going with her. So Letitia thinks I'm after her precious Alice and jumps me on the way to PE. Fucking cat scratched me up to ribbons. Next day Letitia's brought me two roll-ups and a packet of Wrigley's because she's found out the truth and she's sorry. You got to laugh, ent you? (*Slight pause.*)

A bird come in recreation today, bashed itself against the windows like a mad thing. Donna reckons there's loads of 'em trapped in the walls. You can hear 'em.

Lou changes her position but doesn't speak.

Come on, cheer up. It may never happen. (*Slight pause.*) Joke.

You should see all the shit me and Zoë's got past the kangas. She reckons they turn a blind eye 'cos we're all more manageable when we're zombified. We're sitting on a fucking goldmine. Anything you want, just ask and I'll get it for you.

(*With no response from Lou, she starts to answer herself back.*) Lisa's been sent down the block again. 'She hasn't. What's she gone and done now?' Attacked one of the kangas. 'She didn't.' She did. 'Never.' On my life. You'd a thought she'd learnt her lesson last time. 'She's always in trouble that one.' I know. She'll come to a bad end. (*Slight pause.*) Joke.

Lou turns away from Allie.

You're selfish, do you know that? Do you think that you're the only one who doesn't get a visit? The only one who doesn't get phone calls? At least you get letters. Home is a long way away for all of us.

I know what you're doing. You're sucking all my energy up into your silence. You can't do that. The rules are different here. Don't you understand? There isn't enough pity to go round.

(*She turns away from Lou.*) When I was ten I started getting sharp pains in my side and had to be taken to the doctors. Where does it hurt? Here, here or here? His fingers were cold where they touched – no, prodded – me. His pokes left little indentations all over my body because there was no life in my skin. His touch felt like love or as close to it as I could imagine. His touch stayed with me long after the pain had gone and I longed for it. If I concentrated hard enough I could make the pain appear by an effort of will. It became the mystery of our street. I was so obviously not faking it and yet no one could find the reason for the pain. It was the first time I'd got one over on them. They wanted me to hurt because healing me gave them a reason to live, a reason to continue to believe in themselves. Sometimes when the doctor was examining me I felt our roles were reversed and that I was prodding his tummy, listening for his irregular heartbeat and when our gazes met – one cold stare meeting another – I could see that he was aware that I knew.

Lou turns away from Allie.

Bette on E wing does healing. Perhaps you ought to see her. I heard she healed Mandy. Who tried to kill herself? She placed her hand over Mandy's wrist where there was a deep gash and a light come out of her palm and everybody who was there swears they saw the light enter the wound which closed itself up. Now it's as smooth as a newborn baby's. Where does it hurt? Here, here or here?

SCENE FOURTEEN

Lyla's house in Jamaica. The sounds of children playing outside. Bridie stands in the doorway holding a paper shopping bag. Lyla is engaged in an obsessive sweeping of the floor.

Bridie You know, every now and then, just to remind myself of what it feels like, I'll carry something through. That's what I did the day Lou got caught. I had the stuff hidden under my wig. Imagine. All the way over on the plane I had an itchy scalp but I couldn't risk drawing the air hostess's attention to the fact that I was wearing a wig, so I just had to grin and bear it. What's worse, I started to get itchy all over. Nerves I suppose. It could have been any one of us. An unfortunate quirk of fate. I don't suppose she mentions me in any of her letters?

Lyla You better watch you car. Them youth them vicious round here.

Bridie I have a driver sitting in it. I was born here, remember.

Lyla (*still sweeping, calls outside*) Play gentle children.

Bridie I didn't even know that you had children. You look far too young.

Lyla Is me neighbour's children.

Bridie You're not telling me that all those children have the same mother? I suppose motherhood must be an achievement round here. She deserves a medal.

Lyla We all take turns looking after them. Them mother disappear.

Bridie What do you mean? Mothers don't disappear.

Lyla She was a higgler, go off on a shopping trip to restock. Nobody see or hear from her since.

Bridie And nobody knows where she is? What a mystery.

Lyla (*accusatory*) I have a damn good idea where she is.

Bridie (*putting the shopping bag down*) If I'd known about the children I'd have brought more chocolate. It's

58

supposed to be a substitute for a mother's love, isn't it?

Lyla sweeps.

I'm not very good at shopping. I tend not to cook for myself. You know what it's like living out of a suitcase. It's not much – just a few cans of corned beef, rice, some sweets. A little token to prove that I haven't abandoned you. Or Lou. She's going to be all right, you know. It's not so bad in those places. At least you know where she is, three square meals a day and, let me assure you, she's probably safer in there than you are out here. You understand that I can't visit her, don't you? It wouldn't be expedient. Anyway, it's you that I'm worried about. Are you looking after yourself? Eating properly? Working? You can't underestimate the importance of work at times like these.

Lyla continues to sweep the already swept floor.

You can't punish me for ever. One day you'll realize that I was the best friend you ever had. You're acting as though I betrayed you and here I am going out of my way to make sure that you don't starve. I'll take care of you. You need a job. Don't look at me like that. This'll be the equivalent of a desk job. You'd like that wouldn't you? This friend of mine owns a plantation and he's always looking for people to work on it. It's safe, easy work.

Lyla (*stops sweeping*) Me never tell you say me nuh eat corned beef? I never eat food out a tin. Only animal what eat food out a tin a dog. All the meat we eat round here is fresh. You never see the fowl out a yard? Fresh egg every single day. We used to good, healthy food, food like you could buy in any posh hotel restaurant.

Bridie This isn't charity. It's just a small token of my appreciation for your sister's sacrifice.

Lyla Sacrifice? That what you call it?

Bridie You know what I mean.

Lyla You don't have to stuff up my mouth with chocolate to stop me talking to the police. I lived here all my life. I know the rules.

Bridie I'm glad to hear it.

Lyla So tell me, Bridie, why did you choose Lou?

Bridie doesn't reply.

After she get catch me come home and me find out that three other Jamaican girls get catch on the same flight, at least twelve girls get through like me. You did make us think that we was going through by weself. Them other girls was wearing clothes you did buy for them, shoes you pick out. All a them like Lou: them all think that they was your special friend, your sister. Is you tell customs, ennit? Is why you pick out them clothes. You could afford to lose four girls as long as the rest us pass through easy with the bulk of the drugs. Why you didn't choose me for decoy, Bridie? You know what it like when you hear you sister crying out because she get stop at the airport? You know what it like when you can't stop and help her? When you can't even look back? When you have to get on the plane even though her screams ringing in your ears? *(calling out to children outside)* Dennis, what me tell you 'bout playing rough. Don't make me . . . *(getting up)* I'm going to fix that child, so help me.

Lyla goes outside. Bridie looks around the house which, it is obvious, she doesn't feel comfortable in. Lyla returns carrying a toy gun.

Time after time I tell that boy to play gentle with the girls. Look what him have a push in them belly.

Bridie Calm down. It's just a toy.

Lyla Next thing you know him a ride into the community with gang like a pack a cowboy. Why can't the children just play? I sick a this rarted fucking place.

Bridie It's a toy, a harmless toy. See.

She grabs the gun from Lyla and holds it to Lyla's head. She squeezes the trigger. The gun fires quietly. Lyla is subdued.

(*collecting her things together*) You'll have a way to travel to work each day, although you could pick up the little minibus that Cooper lays on for his employees. The pay won't be as good as when you were working for me, but better than for most jobs you'd get round here. That is, if you could find anything round here. I'll come back in a couple of weeks to finalize the details. I'll bring more food.

Bridie goes. Lyla sits. After a moment she picks up the can of corned beef, opens it and eats straight from the can, hungrily.

SCENE FIFTEEN

Allie and Lou's prison cell. Lou lies on her bed as before. Allie jumps onto Lou's bed.

Allie Wake up, Lou. Quick, quick, get up. This is an emergency. It's come. It's finally arrived.

Lou sits up, rubbing her eyes as though she had been asleep.

Look. Look, there. You can't miss it, are you blind? A bird, look.

Allie points into space. Lou looks quizzically but, of course, sees nothing.

Isn't that the most magnificent creature you've ever seen in your life? One of those feathers would be worth – what? A thousand pounds, if you could dare to pluck it out without being trampled. (*She reaches out with her hand but then quickly draws it back.*) It might peck me to death. (*She reaches out again. This time she feels secure enough to stroke it. We can tell that this is a giant bird.*) Oh God, that feels good. Oh God. Oh God. Like lying on your mother's tit when you were a baby. (*She cocks her head.*) Have a listen.

We hear the sound of a bird warbling.

(*laughs*) It tickles. Go on.

Lou cocks her head. She giggles too.

Oh don't go, Mr Dove. Neither of us has had a visitor since we come in here. Look, Lou, he wants us to get on.

Allie and Lou stay on the bed, kneeling. Allie is still behind Lou with her arms around Lou's waist. Although they bob slowly up and down as if flying they do not literally mime the flight which takes place in their minds.

Steady. (*to Lou*) How does that feel? Hold tight. Where's he taking us? Not so fast. We'll fall off. Oh God, the kangas. Hit a kanga we'll end up in the block. Where's the brakes? Too late. Squash.

Lou Splat.

Allie Where are you taking us? Where's he taking us? Hold on. D wing. Cells 15–50 across the corridor, H wing, up the spiral staircase, along another corridor, E wing, down the spiral staircase, through the big swing doors across the green. F block.

Lou Fuckers and farts.

Allie (*speaking more rapidly*) Cells 15–50 across the corridor heading the other way H-wing, up the spiral staircase, along a corridor, E wing, through the swing doors across the green heading anticlockwise to C wing –

Lou Cunts and candlesticks.

Allie Cells 8–80 up the spiral staircase, along the corridor through the green swing doors education, English English English, art, needlework and crafts, computer sciences. Through the green swing doors, down the spiral staircase across the corridor, H block.

Lou Through the green swing doors. Through to the gym, blowing over the girls in the step class with the wind as he runs past. On, on.

Allie Crashing through the locked doors, through to the other side, through to the reception area.

Lou Have you proof of identity? Should you be on this floor?

Allie Bursting through the glass door. Through to the other side. Out.

Lou Out, out, out.

Allie Out onto Parkhurst Road. Out into the parallel universe.

Lou The colour of the city . . . diesel fumes, dogshit, sun-dried piss: sweet perfume.

Allie We coulda got off there and then, hopped on a bus or something but, before we realized what had happened, the bird had left the ground. Uh-oh. That sinking feeling. Like going up in a lift.

Lou Uh oh.

Allie Rising, rising. Floating up till Holloway Road was a thin silver worm.

Lou Higher and higher.

Allie Wind blowing our faces from the great bird's wings.

Lou Higher and higher.

Allie Above the clouds.

Lou Windless. Silent.

Allie Moving swiftly through London's different zones.

Lou Up, up, up.

Allie Land disappears.

Lou Across water.

Allie Day and night passing us in seconds. Time passing quickly with the miles.

Lou Where he taking us?

Allie Because the flight seemed purposeful.

The women's movements suddenly stop.

Then he stopped, hovering over a vast expanse of ocean. And that's where we stayed.

Lou For three days and three nights.

Allie The colour of the water changing with the light, first heavy, grey like thundered glass, then inky and dark as our souls.

Lou First heavy, grey like thundered glass, then inky and dark as our souls. Changing, changing and always the same.

Allie We hovered for three days and nights watching the water change.

Lou And then we understood.

Allie Everything.

Sound of a succession of heavy prison doors clanging shut and keys turning in locks.

London.
Bridie is curled up on the ground. Her dress is torn and there is blood on her face. Sammie and Rog are beside her. Bridie doesn't move. Sammie takes a handkerchief out of her pocket and starts to clean Bridie up.

Rog We ought to call an ambulance.

Sammie No need. It's not that bad.

Rog She's losing blood.

Sammie They're superficial wounds. She'll live.

Rog You're an expert, are you?

Sammie She wouldn't want us to get anyone else involved.

Rog It'll be your fault if she bleeds to death.

Sammie It's stopping already, look.

Rog Who did this to her?

Sammie Best not to ask questions, eh?

Rog What did she do wrong?

Sammie Life isn't all cause and effect, Rog.

Rog It's a warning isn't it?

Sammie Good way as any of motivating your staff, I suppose.

Rog How can you be so cool about it? It could have been

any one of us.

Sammie No use crying over spilt milk, is there? Help me get her up.

Rog I don't think I can hack it, Sammie.

Sammie No? Then why don't you go home?

Rog Just leave her here?

Sammie I'll take care of her. I've seen it all before. Go on, go home.

Rog I can't. You know I can't.

Sammie laughs, continues to clean Bridie up with the tissue.

Sammie Why? Seen a Nicole Farhi you fancy? Or a pair of shoes in a glossy magazine that a girl in Tesco's would have to save six months for? You got nothing to go home for, have you?

Rog I wanted to be just like her.

Sammie But not any more?

Rog I don't know what she is.

Sammie I doubt whether she even knows herself. Take away the false passports, the clothes, the hair extensions, nails – what have you got left? Haven't you ever been beaten up, Rog?

Rog Never.

Sammie It's like losing your virginity. Once you've experienced it you lose your fear of it. Like the first time I had an accident in my car. By rights I should have died but I got up and walked away and after that I wasn't afraid of anything. You don't think she just laid back and took it, do you? She'd look a darn sight prettier if she hadn't fought back.

Rog They could have killed her.

Sammie By rights she should have died years ago. She's gone beyond fear and why shouldn't she? Don't you get tired of being told that you mustn't answer back, mustn't go out after dark?

Rog Just think, I used to be scared of her.

Sammie She's intelligent. Gifted. A match for any man. How does a woman like her get on in the world? This is the only life she knows.

Rog She's nothing but a mule.

Sammie Come on, help me get her into bed.

They begin to move Bridie.

I've seen a painting I want. Only I've nowhere to put it. Perhaps I'll give it to you, as a present. Who knows, it might start you on a whole new hobby.

SCENE SEVENTEEN

Jamaica. Three years later.
Lyla is working in a field. She carries a baby on her back. Lou enters and stands, unseen, watching her.

Lyla Hush, hush nuh baby. Soon come. Mummy soon come and baby and mummy can have a nice cool drink. Just a few more minutes then we can have a nice long rest. (*She looks across the field. She smiles.*) They got that woman working out here again. The one who lost her mind. Why they give her work again? Don't laugh baby, it isn't funny. She doing the best she can.

Lou So this is where you working.

Lyla turns around.

Lyla Lou. What are you doing here?

Lou I follow you.

Lyla I can see that. Well?

Lou You say you got job in a hotel. You say you leave baby with a minder and do waitressing.

Lyla Why you follow me?

Lou I didn't believe you.

Lyla I got to work, Lou.

Lou In a ganja field?

Lyla You find me another job and I will take it. You can find me another job?

Lou But a ganja field? After everything we been through?

Lyla What else can I do, Lou?

Lou How much they paying you?

Lyla Twenty US dollar a week.

Lou You can live without that, might as well be working for free.

Lyla Everybody got to work, Lou. It's better than nothing.

Lou And the baby? Why you didn't leave her with me?

Lyla I didn't think you want to look after her.

Lou Of course I would look after her.

Lyla (*stops work*) You never look at her.

Lou You finish now?

Lyla Lunch break. Want some?

Lyla takes out some bread that she has wrapped up. She breaks it and gives a piece to Lou who eats.

Lou What about Shaneka?

Lyla She sleeping. Is the heat, thank God. Imagine working and looking after baby at the same time.

Lou They don't mind you bringing her?

Lyla As long as I get on with the work. She ain't no trouble to them. *(holds her arms out)* Oh, a little breeze. Don't that feel good, Lou, a little breeze on your skin? Look at them children playing in the next field. Remember when we used to play like that?

Lou I know what you trying to do, Lyla.

Lyla This is the first time you come outa the house since you get back, Lou. You just been locked away for four years. Why you want to lock yourself up again? Is it shame? All the neighbours know what happen, Lou, and none of them would blame you for it. Since you come back you ain't even said a word about what happen to you in England.

Lou takes the baby from the shawl tied to Lyla's back and comforts it.

Lou What a pretty girl. What a plump pretty girl.

Lyla Everybody say she favour me.

Lou Favour you to death. Funny, Lyla, when I come back everything, everybody change up. You change. Time move on for you. Two kids, a new man, work, but for me time stop the minute I enter that building. I feel like I was robbed and I know I shouldn't feel that way, Lyla, because of what I done, but that's how I feel. What I got to go outside for? Any jobs outside? Any food?

69

Lyla You out now, Lou, you out in the open.

Lou You ever see Bridie?

Lyla No, I never see Bridie.

Lou Every day I wait for a letter from Bridie. Every day I wait for a visit from Bridie. Bridie disappear. Bridie putting her foot up in a posh hotel. I hate Bridie.

Lyla Every day you was away I think about waiting in the queue and hearing you screaming behind me. Getting onto the plane without looking back. I'm sorry, Lou. Sorry, sorry, sorry.

Lou Is not your fault, Lyla.

Lyla I wish it was me them catch.

Lou I don't want you to feel sorry for me. I can't feel sorry for meself.

Lyla Let's go out tonight. Curl up we hair, put on make-up, put on we best clothes and go a dancehall.

Lou Wine up weself and have a good time.

Lyla Make way for the dancehall queens.

Lou Watching all the young boys a pump an' grind.

Lyla An' if I'm lucky one a them might kiss me.

Lou Nobody touch me in four years.

The women hug each other.

Lyla Is over now, Lou, all over. You home. You free. You can start all over again.

Lou Every day I thought about you, carry your picture to bed to help me sleep, think about home.

Lyla An' now you never have to leave again.

Lou Never leave again. (*cradles baby*) You have your mother's eyes and her smile. Strong little fingers – you have her strength too. I wish you beauty and intelligence. I hope that you will travel to far away lands. I wish you the power of flight. (*to Lyla*) I still think about Bridie.

Lyla Why?

Lou Because she was the only person I ever meet in me life who offered me hope.

Lyla Some hope, Lou.

Lou Who else give us a job? Who else take us shopping in London? We will never have these things again.

Lyla (*looking out across the field*) Oh my God, look at her, that madwoman. Why they put somebody like that to work in a field? (*laughing*) Oh my God, she doing the dance a the cutlass.

Lou (*laughing*) She going chop off her own head. You sure she ain't been smoking the weed herself?

Lyla She been smoking something.

The women look out across the field, laughing. Suddenly Lou stops laughing.

Lou We will never leave the ghetto.

Lyla Come on, Lou, you going to help me finish this piece a work so that we can go home early or you just going to stand and look?

Lou takes a cutlass and starts to chop. The women chop in silence. As Lyla works, Lou stops and watches her for a while and then looks out across the field. Lyla looks up at her and Lou starts to work again. They both continue to work in silence, without looking at each other, as the lights go down.

71